# Unravel Emotions

## A Journey Through the Depths of Feeling

Pratiksha Kumbhare

BookLeaf
Publishing

India | USA | UK

# Dedication

To those who feel deeply,
May you find comfort in the chaos,
Clarity in the confusion,
And courage in every unspoken truth.

This book is for the hearts that ache, the minds that wonder, and the souls that seek to unravel the beauty within every emotion.

# Preface

So here I am...compelled to give words to my thoughts and emotions. Here I am ready to express my feelings, take charge of my emotions and explore the beauty of every feeling. Writing something on emotions seems like I am taking my heart and soul out in the world. But it feels so right that I don't fear of any judgments. Unravel Emotions is my happy place to share my thoughts about emotions and life.

# Acknowledgements

*To my loving husband, Deepesh for his unwavering support that fuels my dreams.*

*To my parents who gifted me wings to soar high.*

*To my in-laws for their unconditional love and encouragement.*

*To my younger brother, Prateek, my brothers in law Ankit and Himanshu, my pillars of strength.*

*To my best friend, Priya who stands by me through every high and low.*

*And last but not least, to my precious son whose arrival inspired me to write.*

*This book is a tribute to each of you, for shaping my journey with love and belief.*

# 1. Unraveling Emotions

*Here I stand with words untold,*
*Pouring thoughts so raw, so bold.*
*No fear, no chains to hold me tight,*
*Just heart and soul in open light.*

*Each feeling deep, I set it free,*
*A glimpse of what's inside of me.*
*Through every joy, through every pain,*
*I write, I heal, I breathe again.*

*This is my place, my sacred space,*
*Where emotions find their time and grace.*
*For happiness is not a chase,*
*But self-love's warm and kind embrace.*

# 2. The Joy of Childhood

Oh, what a time was childhood bright,
No worries to weigh, no troubles in sight.
Just laughter pure and moments free,
A joyful mess of endless glee.

A heartfelt laugh, a selfless share,
No hidden thoughts, just love and care.
A time to dream with boundless grace,
To roam so free in time's embrace.

# 3. The Storm of Adolescence

A shifting form, a restless mind,
Emotions tangled, hard to unwind.
A heart that races, doubts that grow,
Fear and confusion start to show.

With every change, the tides arise,
Mood swings dance like cloudy skies.
Dreams and pressure, side by side,
A winding path, a storm to ride.

# 4. The Path to Triumph

With toil and grit, the strong arise,
through sleepless nights and endless tries.
Each failure whispers, "Try once more,"
a hidden key to open doors.

The taste of victory, rich and sweet,
a fleeting spark yet hard to keep.
Step beyond where comfort lies,
and watch the world applaud your rise.

But tread with wisdom, choose with care,
for success can build or strip you bare.
Rise with honor, stand your ground,
let triumph lift, not pull you down.

# 5. Inseparable Souls

I found a friend, a soul so dear
A sister's heart forever near.
She knows my joys, my hidden fears,
The unspoken words, the falling tears.

With just "Hello," she hears it all
The rise, the ache, the silent fall.
A keeper of secrets, wild and free,
My partner in every sweet memory.

No miles, no time can pull apart
The threads we've woven, heart to heart.
Through wins and losses, smiles and pain,
Our bond stays strong, will never wane.

From days when no one knew or cared,
Through every moment, we have shared.
A friendship true, a timeless blend
A sister found in my best friend.

# 6. Young Love

I remember the spark, the gaze, the touch,
The smile that lingered, the fear, too much.
They say love ripens, like fine wine with time,
But young love's rhythm still beats in my mind.

It was wild, it was pure, like a rising flame,
A whisper of magic, a heart unchained.
Seasons may fade, but memories stay
That first sweet love won't drift away.

It was fresh, it was bold, and it felt so true,
A feeling that changed me, a light that still grew.
Though years may pass, and the seasons may part,
That first love still lives in the depths of my heart.

# 7. Love in Separation

Oh, she loved him deep, intense,
A love so wild, so immense.
He was her dream, her breath, her night,
Her sweetest sin, her purest light.

His touch, his kiss, his whispered name,
Set her soul and skin aflame.
They lived in moments, raw and true,
A love they both so deeply knew.

He swore he'd never let her cry,
Yet left her drowning, asking why.
Still, when his name drifts through the air,
Her heart skips beats she's still aware.

Apart they stand, yet love remains,
A quiet ache, a sweet refrain.
For love can bloom where distance lies,
Like stars that shine in separate skies.

# 8. She Rises

Shredded by love, yet steady she stands,
No heartbreak can weaken her hands.
Eyes on the prize, her vision burns bright,
Chasing her dreams through day and night.

She shines like gold no shadow can hide,
In storms of pain, she turns with pride.
She knows her worth no tear will remain,
She buries the past and breaks every chain.

A force, unyielding, fierce and true,
With every step, she starts anew.
Now crowned with skill, she claims her place,
A queen of her field, full of grace.

The world will watch as she ascends,
Her story of triumph never ends.

# 9. Timeless Love

In a world where love drifts away,
Ours still feels like yesterday.
Through every rise, through every fall,
Our hearts beat strong we've had it all.

From whispered dreams to battles fought,
Through joy and tears, the lessons taught.
No pride, no walls, no need to prove,
Just endless trust, just boundless love.

Through every storm, through every tide,
We stand as one, side by side.
Two hearts that fate made whole
Forever one, a single soul.

# 10. My Everything

You came to me, a gift so true,
A piece of me, my soul in you.
With every breath, with every sigh,
My heart is yours no reason why.

I'm lost in you, I'm found the same,
Forever bound, a love untamed.
Oh, my baby, my shining light,
My sun by day, my moon at night.

Your tiny hands, your wobbly stride,
Each little word fills me with pride.
You are my world, my heart, my whole,
My precious child, my very soul.

# 11. A Mother's Heart

I see her laughing, hand in hand,
With her little one in the golden sand.
No hurried calls, no rushed goodbyes,
Just endless time 'neath open skies.

She soaks in every fleeting day,
While I must watch mine slip away.
Duty calls, the hours steal,
A longing ache I cannot heal.

She walks beside each step, each fall,
She answers every childish call.
No stolen moments, torn in two
Her world is whole, unlike mine too.

Oh, how I wish for time so free,
To give my child the whole of me.
Yet love endures, though time is small,
For a mother's heart still gives its all.

# 12. Tolerance

Tolerance, a word so wide,
Endurance, strength, the will to bide.
To bear the weight, to stand so tall,
To face the storm and take it all.

To understand, to let things be,
To grant beliefs that disagree.
Yet deep beneath, the truth remains,
Tolerance often nurtures pain.

For women, more when vows are tied,
It means the tears they push aside.
Not just patience, not just grace,
But silent wounds they must embrace.

# 13. Break the Chain

We are but slaves to thoughts we weave,
Bound by chains we can't unleave.
Right and wrong, we clearly see,
Yet change remains a distant plea.

Our minds take charge, they lead the way,
We follow them, we go astray.
But once we learn to break their hold,
A new horizon will unfold.

# 14. Inner Conflict

The world, they say, is dark and cold,
A place of sorrow, harsh and old.
Yet few will see, or dare to find,
The deepest battles lie inside.

Our fiercest foe is not the land,
But thoughts that slip from our own hand.
For when we tame the storm within,
A brighter world will then begin.

# 15. Empathy

Her silent curse,
She feels the pain, but never verse.
Not the joy, not the light,
Only sorrow fills her sight.

A stranger's grief, a loved one's ache,
Upon her soul, their burdens break.
She holds their weight, she lets it stay,
And carries hurt day after day.

She longs to be the girl she knew,
Bright, unshaken, pure, and true.
Each day she tries, yet slips again,
A war she fights but can't explain.

Still, she hopes she won't let go,
That strength will rise, her heart will glow.
That one day soon, she'll stand up tall,
And find herself beyond it all.

# 16. Invisible Scars of COVID-19

The world stood still in fear and dread,
As silent tears and prayers were spread.
March arrived, and time stood tight,
The future drowned in endless night.

The streets were bare, the doors were closed,
Jobs were lost, and hope deposed.
Families torn, their laughter ceased,
Love was feared, and touch decreased.

Each ringing phone a pang of fright,
What news would come, what loss that night?
Months went by, yet pain remained,
Invisible wounds, unnamed, unstained.

Years have passed, yet scars persist,
In broken dreams and lives dismissed.
I met my uncle, once so free,
Now bound by fate's cruel decree.

Their business lost, their spirits weak,
A silent grief they do not speak.
The women smile, though hearts may ache,
Their strength the thread that will not break.

But men now drown in guilt and fear,
A burdened soul, a fallen tear.
I see their pain, I feel it deep,
Yet all I do is pray and weep.

Oh, may their hearts find light again,
May joy return, may peace remain.
For those who suffered, those who grieve,
Deserve to heal, deserve relief.

# 17. Silent Suffering

The one you love turns blind to you,
a quiet storm, yet nothing new.
Alive you stand, yet dead within,
a hollow heart where pain begins.

The flowers bright once kissed the sky,
now withered, brittle left to die.
The smile that danced with morning light,
fades away in endless night.

No soul can hear the silent screams,
no eyes can trace the shattered dreams.
Alone, you walk through burning hell,
where love once bloomed but never dwelled.

# 18. Silent Cries

Why does love sometimes fade to cold,
A shadow lost from hands once bold?
Why does a heart turn blank, estranged
A soul once close now feels so changed?

Is love a price that wealth can buy,
A fleeting spark a hollow lie?
When words run dry, and smiles grow thin,
Is gold the glue that holds within?

I bear the ache no eyes can see,
A silent storm that buries me.
When your heart turns and drifts away,
What words are left for me to say?

Is love so weak so bound by greed,
A fragile thing of want, not need?
Yet here I stand, though torn apart,
Chained by hope and a broken heart.

But love, true love, can't be disguised
It lives in souls, not in the prize.
And though I ache in quiet despair,
I still believe real love is rare.

# 19. Lost in the Crowd

Why do I float in a cloud so high,
yet feel so lost beneath the sky?
My home is full, their voices near,
but love feels distant hard to hear.

I have it all, yet feel so bare,
a hollow heart, an empty stare.
Can someone tell me what this means,
why joy feels like forgotten dreams?

Sadness lingers, trust betrayed,
a weary soul in shadows swayed.
Nothing to share, no smile to show,
just silent tears that freely flow.

# 20. Journaling

From a heart that's torn apart,
Music sings a work of art.
Just as sorrow weaves a tune,
Pain finds beauty, late or soon.

Words arise from aching deep,
Lines where hidden heartaches weep.
Turn your sorrow into ink,
Let it flow don't stop to think.

Journals hold the soul's release,
Bringing clarity and peace.
With each word, the pain will fade,
Leaving light where dark was laid.

# 21. The Power of Positivity

A single sparka thought so bright,
Can turn the darkness into light.
One hopeful whisper, soft yet strong,
Can lift your heart and push you along.

When shadows call, just let them fade,
Focus on hope, don't be afraid.
For in your mind, the power lies
A world transformed through brighter eyes.

With thoughts aligned in hues of gold,
No fear can break, no doubt can hold.
You shape your path, you choose to rise
A master of life beneath open skies.

# 22. A Wish for a Miracle

I wish for a miracle, pure and bright,
To chase away this endless night.
To find once more that carefree grace
A smiling heart, a brighter place.

I long to be who I used to know
A soul that sparkled, a heart aglow.
Where laughter danced on winds so free,
And life felt light, as it should be.

Let sorrow fade like shadows fall,
When morning sun breaks through it all.
May pain dissolve, and stress unwind,
Leaving hope and peace to find.

I seek a life both true and kind
Of honest heart and peaceful mind.
A simple path where joy can reign,
No heavy burdens, no more pain.

I wish for a miracle, soft and clear,
To bring back light and draw me near
To days of warmth, where I can see
A world of hope and serenity.

# 23. Threads of Love Through Time

Those were the days when Mom would wake me with
grace,
Soft lullabies and a warm embrace.
Now I rise early, with love in my heart,
To greet my son as a brand-new day starts.

Once I was cradled in their tender care,
With laughter and lessons floating in the air.
Now it's my turn to nurture and guide,
To hold tiny hands and walk by his side.

From a little girl with dreams so wide,
To a proud wife, sharing life with pride.
From a young soul, full of hope and light,
To a mother who kisses her child goodnight.

I once held Dad's finger, strong and near,
A shield of comfort, a heart sincere.
Now I kiss my son's tiny hand with cheer,

And whisper sweet hopes for every new year.

Time flows gently, like a river's song,
Yet in my heart, love keeps me strong.
Through each new chapter, joys intertwine,
A legacy of love that forever shines.

So far, this journey has been a beautiful ride,
A path of love, with family by my side.
Through every season, with arms open wide,
I cherish each moment with heart and pride.

# 24. From Ashes, I Rise like a Phoenix

I leave behind the tears that fell like rain,
The echoes of struggle, the whispers of pain.
With every word, I build a new,
A world of dreams, both bright and true.

Through ink and hope, I seek to shine,
To claim the goals that once were mine.
A chapter turns—a fresh, unknown page,
A heart unbound from sorrow's cage.

One day, I'll glance at where I've been,
At battles fought and truths unseen.
Like a phoenix, I'll soar, fierce and free,
A soul reborn in destiny.

And through it all, God's hand will stay
Guiding my steps, lighting the way.
With love, with faith, I'll always know
I'm never alone as I rise and grow.